Project
Manager

From LinkedIn Experts

Table of Contents

Q1- What is your leadership style?

Project managers help teams set goals and work together effectively. Interviewers ask this question to assess whether you have the leadership skills to build relationships and motivate your colleagues.

Candidate answer and feedback
By Project Manager Professional

I tend to be a very collaborative leader under normal circumstances, but I become more focused and directive when the team is under pressure.

For example, I worked on a project last year where we had to include people from four different parts of the company. Early on, I worked hard to make sure that our meetings were scheduled at convenient times, and that everyone felt welcome as they got added to the project team. But a few months into the project a few of the team members started showing up late for meetings, or missing them altogether.

As a result, we found ourselves slipping behind, and it started to look like we might miss a deadline. I scheduled one-to-one meetings with each person to find out what was going on, and get them to commit to completing their tasks. In one case, the person was just too busy, so we talked to their supervisor and got a different person assigned to our project instead.

In the end, we were able to complete the project on time, and we all formed a real bond from having worked together on that team.

Why this answer worked well:

- The answer provides evidence from practical experience.
- It showed that the candidate can adapt and collaborate to meet the needs of a team and project.
- The candidate included a personal story with a real challenge and positive result.

Answer framework

Focus on balance

This is a chance to talk about yourself, and how you work with other people. As a project manager, you need to balance "influence" and "authority" in order to keep people motivated and get tasks completed.

Adaptability is key

Highlight your flexibility and adaptability by demonstrating that you know there are lots of different ways to lead, and show that you are able to match your leadership style to the needs of your team in different situations. Tell a story that shows how you changed your leadership style to meet a situation.

Tips

- Demonstrate that you can adapt your leadership style to meet the project.
- Show empathy. Project leaders need to look after their people at the same time they are looking after the business.
- Get to know yourself. The LinkedIn Learning course "Project Management Foundations: Teams" explains several different ways to understand yourself and your team members. It also provides links to websites where you can complete your own personality profile.

Q2-Tell me about a time when your team had a challenging deadline to meet.

Project Managers often have to balance multiple tasks and tight timelines, so interviewers want to know that you can work well under pressure. This question will help them understand whether deadlines motivate you to plan things out and get work done, or simply stress you out.

Candidate answer and feedback
By Project Manager Professional

I was on a four-person team in school, and we had to work together to study a problem and deliver a report with recommendations.

The four of us did not know each other well, and we only had a month to finish the project. In order to get things started, I gathered everyone's contact information and got everyone to agree on a time and a place to meet to kick off the project.

When we met face to face, we discussed what it would take to complete the project, and assigned roles and deadlines to the team members. It was a lot of work, especially pulling all of the information together at the end. But we got it done, and we got an A on the project.

That experience taught me about how important it is to get everyone onboard from the beginning of the project to create a plan, and then to make sure that the work is getting done on time.

Why this answer worked well:

- The story was relatable and authentic, which helped the interviewer get to know the candidate.
- The candidate showed that they are a self-starter with the confidence to step up as a leader.
- The answer ended on a positive note, demonstrating personal experience with the value of managing a project well.

Answer framework

Use the STAR-L approach

This approach helps you to give a detailed and thorough answer by checking off each important component of your story.

Situation: Give important and relevant details about the circumstances.

Task: Describe the main duties that you needed to complete.

Action: Outline the steps you took to meet your goals.

Result: Share the quantifiable results of your efforts.

Learning: Detail what you'd repeat or do differently in the future.

Tips

- Make a list of five interesting stories that highlight your best qualities and relevant experience.
- Practice using these stories to answer different questions.
- It's okay to talk about challenges and failures, but emphasize the positive lessons that you and your team members learned.

Q3- Imagine that you're the project manager for a software development team. There are two days left in the current sprint, and your team is not going to be able to deliver all of the features that they had planned. What do you do?

Things don't always go as planned. Interviewers ask this question to assess your ability to track what's really happening, communicate that status professionally to the stakeholders, and keep everyone aligned as the plan evolves and progresses.

Candidate answer and feedback

By Project Manager Professional

In this situation, it sounds like the team underestimated the effort required to deliver some of the features, or had overlooked some challenges.

So the first thing to do is get the information about which features are not going to be completed, and why. Maybe they underestimated the work, the team got pulled away for another project, or someone got sick. It would also be good to see which features are going to be completed. Then, this information needs to be shared with the product manager because the product manager is typically the sponsor for Agile teams.

The product manager may decide to eliminate some features, if they don't provide enough value to justify the effort. Or, the product manager may reprioritize the order in which the features will be developed.

Since there was clearly a gap in the planning early on, it might be good for the product manager to meet directly with the team to make sure they're getting everyone's input into the decision, and reducing the risk of being overly optimistic again. Once they've revised the plan, they may need to update other stakeholders such as sales and marketing, or their customers.

Why this answer worked well:

- The candidate started by understanding the situation and exploring possible causes for the delay.
- The candidate engaged the team and the product manager to come up with a solution.
- Communication was central, as the candidate shared the changes and the new plan to the affected stakeholders.

Answer framework

Detail your process

A common challenge for project managers is that things won't always go as planned. You want to explain how you would use a process for gathering the facts, evaluating the options, engaging your stakeholders, and then making the necessary changes to your plan.

Showcase your technical knowledge

Consider ways to incorporate technical understanding and proficiencies into your answer. For example, if you're discussing a sprint, you can use the opportunity to show off your knowledge of the Agile methodology.

Tips

- Highlight your understanding of the balance between scope, schedule, and budget — that if you change one of them it will probably affect the others.
- Demonstrate that you expect things to change once a plan is underway. This shows your tendency to manage the changes smoothly, rather than ignoring them or allowing them to become a crisis.
- Focus on communication and share that you always engage the team and their stakeholders to revise a plan.

Q4- Tell me about a time when things didn't go as you had planned.

During projects, the unexpected happens all the time, so the interviewer wants to know how you're going to react when things take a turn. By asking you to describe how you've dealt with surprises in the past, they're actually trying to understand how you'll react to surprises in the future.

Candidate answer and feedback
By Project Manager Professional

Last year, I was assigned to a project to select a new customer relationship management (CRM) system for the company. We analyzed the different options, and selected the best one for our team.

But once we started working on the implementation, I discovered that our new CRM wasn't compatible with our transportation management system (TMS). I realized that we had a few choices. We could stop implementing the new CRM system, we could change the TMS to one that was compatible, we could implement a third system act as a bridge, or just deal with having two systems that couldn't communicate with each other.

I met with our project sponsor to help her make a decision. She decided that the best option was to move forward with the implementation. And then, as soon as it was up and running, we could turn our focus to upgrading the TMS. While it would have been better to discover this compatibility issue sooner, the outcome would likely have been the same. Ultimately, the two upgrades improved our efficiency and made it easier to take care of our customers.

That project taught me a lot about the value of planning ahead and trying to anticipate potential challenges. And it also taught me how important it is to work together as a team to come up with the best solutions.

Why this answer worked well:

- The candidate used the STAR-L system to tell a story, explaining the challenges and the positive outcomes, including lessons learned.
- The answer included a little bit of industry-specific detail, without getting deep into the technical jargon. Even someone who hasn't worked with CRM or TMS systems can understand the basic problem of having two computer programs that don't communicate.
- The candidate demonstrated that success was dependent on their individual actions and contributions, as well as the way that they interacted as a part of the team.

Answer framework

Be honest, but find the positives

This can be a tricky question, because you have to tell a story about a situation that might be negative. You want to tell the story honestly, but you also want to highlight the positive outcomes such as learning and resilience.

Use the STAR-L approach

This approach helps you to give a detailed and thorough answer by checking off each important component of your story.

Situation: Give important and relevant details about the circumstances.

Task: Describe the main duties that you needed to complete.

Action: Outline the steps you took to meet your goals.

Result: Share the quantifiable results of your efforts.

Learning: Detail what you'd repeat or do differently in the future.

Tips

- Reveal your personal style and behaviors within the context of the situation you're describing.
- Limit the use of technical jargon to avoid appearing condescending or too focused on irrelevant details.
- Be candid about challenges, but always emphasize positive outcomes and growth moments.

Q5- Imagine that you are managing a construction project. You've just been notified that the construction site is flooded because of a severe storm. What do you do next?

Project managers sometimes need to respond quickly when there's an emergency. Interviewers will ask this sort of question to see whether you can think through your options quickly, and make decisions.

Candidate answer and feedback

By Project Manager Professional

Rain is a common problem for construction schedules, so I would want to be prepared for this possibility ahead of time.

There are three things that I'd need to focus on. The first is safety and making sure everyone is okay. Second, I'd need to consider how this circumstance affects the scope, schedule, and budget for the project. The third thing is communication. I would reach out to the people on the project team and all other stakeholders, and let them know what is happening.

Everyone is going to want to know how the flooding will affect them, so I would anticipate their questions and have answers ready. For example, people are likely to ask, "How will this affect the schedule for my tasks?" Or, "How long will this delay the completion of the project?" Updating the project plan will make it much easier to answer these questions.

As more information becomes available, I would set in place a simple way to update the stakeholders. I'd consider email, Slack, Teams, or an internal site with Frequently Asked Questions.

Why this answer worked well:

- The answer outlined the candidate's ability to solve problems in high-pressure situations.
- The candidate showed a commitment to safety.
- The candidate detailed what was required to change the plan, including communication to all stakeholders.

Answer framework

Focus on your process

Surprises happen all the time during projects, and you need to help your teams be flexible and adaptable. Detail how you'd go about gathering facts, analyzing risks, communicating with stakeholders, and keeping everyone working together as things change.

Share how you rally the team

Your answer should show that you understand that some surprises are unavoidable, and rather than trying to place blame, a Project Manager needs to figure out what the impacts will be and keep all of the stakeholders engaged.

Tips

- Focus on a few categories of actions and explain them in order. This helps you maintain your train of thought, and it's easier for the interviewer to follow along.
- Link your recommendations to the priorities of the company that you are interviewing with.

Q6- Imagine that I'm a senior executive who is sponsoring your project, and you are the project manager. I have just told you that the company is cutting budgets, and we need to trim 10% from the cost of your project. What should you do next?

Budget cuts can be an unfortunate reality for many businesses, especially when the economy changes or when new leaders come onboard. Interviewers ask this question to see how you react to bad news, and whether you are able to keep focused on finding the best ways to support the business, even as things change.

Candidate answer and feedback

By Project Manager Professional

Cost-cutting happens all the time in business, so the first thing is to make sure that the whole team understands that it isn't personal.

Then, we need to remember that projects are a balance between scope, schedule, and budget. So, if the budget needs to be cut, we'll probably need to decide whether we can stretch the project out over a longer time, and save money that way. Or, whether there is scope that we can remove from the project.

In other words, are there some things that we can decide not to do because they are less important?

Once the team is able to come up with a new plan that fits the lower budget, we need to revise the schedule and the budget, get the changes approved, and communicate those changes to everyone who will be affected.

Why this answer worked well:

- The answer showed that the candidate's first priority is doing what is right for the business.

- The candidate demonstrated an understanding of how to make trade-offs between scope, schedule, and budget.
- The candidate showed that they're aware of how changes will affect a team.

Answer framework

Align your actions with their needs

For this question, think about the challenge that the interviewer is dealing with, and how your actions will help them achieve their goals.

Focus on flexibility and leadership

This is an opportunity to demonstrate your business acumen and demonstrate an understanding of the bigger picture. Reassure the interviewer of your ability to help your whole team adapt to changes.

Tips

- Think about this question from an executive's point of view and how your actions could help them.
- Show that you can defend the project and team while also doing what's best for the business.

Q7- Tell me about a time you managed a project.

Interviewers can ask this question as a way to break the ice and give you a chance to talk about your experience as a Project Manager. Your answer will give them evidence about how ready you are to jump in and start managing projects in their organization. It can also give them ideas for follow-up questions about things that you mention, or about things that you leave out.

Last year, I went on a trip to Europe with five of my friends and I volunteered to be the project manager. I had to get everyone's input about where they thought we should go, what we should see, and how much money we should spend on transportation and lodging.

Then, I needed to make sure everyone had the information they needed so that they could arrange their passports, their visas, and buy their tickets. In order to make sure we didn't miss any steps, I created a work breakdown structure with all of the tasks, and then mapped out the timeline using a Gantt chart.

I also created a risk register where I tracked issues that we were concerned about, from someone getting sick to countries changing their visa requirements. I used a free online program that sent reminders out about the tasks that each of us needed to complete, and then I sent out weekly status reports to the whole team right up until the day that we left.

The trip was awesome! But we did run into a few surprises that we hadn't expected. So, when we got back, I spent a little time writing down the lessons that I learned from the project, and the things that I would do differently next time.

Why this answer worked well:

- The candidate explained the key steps in project management, and familiarity with the tools and techniques.

- By using a personal example, the candidate showed how project management applies to daily life.
- The answer showed that the candidate is a natural team leader and shared an interest in travel.
- The story gave the interviewer a lot of options for follow-up questions to get to know the candidate better.

Answer framework

Show your understanding of principles

This is an opportunity to show that you understand how the principles of project management apply to lots of different situations. We all work on projects every day, but project managers understand what it takes to run those projects efficiently.

Share a professional success

One possible approach is to give a straight answer and talk about a project that's similar to the work you would be doing with the company. For example, a project that you did in school, or with a previous employer.

Make it personal

You could also use an example from an aspect of your personal life, such as a hobby or volunteer work. This tack provides the interviewer with the information they need about your project management skills, but also gives them a better appreciation for your personality.

Tips

- Choose an example that is closely related to the job, or one that highlights something about your personality.
- Focus on explaining how you used project management tools and techniques to help the team plan, execute, and close out the project.

Q8- How have you measured the results of your past projects?

Business people love to talk about metrics, because measurement is an essential part of management. The interviewer might ask this question to see how comfortable you are with measuring the results of your work. They may also want to see how well you can connect operational metrics (such as completing a project on time) back to business goals (like return on investment).

Candidate answer and feedback
By Project Manager Professional

Last year, I was part of a project team that updated our company's online storefront to make it more stylish and easier to use.

At the beginning, our team did stakeholder interviews and customer surveys to collect our requirements. We used the requirements to create a project plan and a budget. During the project, we had weekly scrum meetings where we tracked which tasks had been completed. That gave us internal metrics to ensure we stayed on schedule and within our budget.

When we were done with development, we compared the finished website against our original requirements to ensure that we delivered 100 percent of the scope that we'd been given. We surveyed customers and found their level of satisfaction increased by 35% with the new site.

Last, but definitely not least, the online store generated a 75% sales increase, which meant we returned on the investment in just two months. So, we used a combination of project metrics, customer metrics, and business metrics to make sure we were doing the right things in the right way.

Why this answer worked well:

- The answer included an example that most people can relate to. A little bit technical, but not too much.

- The candidate used a variety of internal and external metrics to judge project performance.
- Including metrics like revenue and customer satisfaction showed why the project was relevant for the business.

Answer framework

Use external and internal metrics

Projects should be aligned with the goals of a business, and there are lots of ways to measure their performance. Use external metrics if the project delivered the results that were expected, such as improving customer service, increasing revenue, or decreasing costs. Use internal metrics to track whether the project is on time and on budget, when compared to the plan.

Share a relevant example

Depending on your experience, you might be able to give specific examples of the external and internal metrics that you used to evaluate a project. Otherwise, you can talk more generally about the aspects of the project to which you and your colleagues were paying the most attention.

Tips

- Try to reference metrics that are most important to the company, like efficiency or business impact.
- Be prepared to describe specific metrics such as Return on Investment, Net Present Value, Earned Value, and others.

Q9- What sorts of things get you excited, and make you enjoy work?

We all tend to do a better job when we like the work that we are doing. Interviewers want to know whether you enjoy doing the work that's required to manage their projects effectively. They'll be looking to see if you like interacting with people, whether you're methodical about planning, and if you enjoy learning new things.

Candidate answer and feedback

By Project Manager Professional

I really enjoy working on teams to solve hard challenges. I don't always need to be the center of attention, but I'm not afraid to speak up and ask questions.

It's fun to think through scenarios and come up with creative ideas. It also helps team members get to know each other better by seeing how different people think and communicate their ideas. This kind of collaboration can also help teams bond and build trust. The best part is that it's really rewarding when you can see how the little things you do here and there contributed to making a big change.

When teams work well together, they can do so much more than any contributor can accomplish alone. And that's the thing that gets me most excited — being part of a team that gets things done well.

Why this answer worked well:

- The candidate connected their passions to what they'd be doing regularly in the job — and we all tend to perform better when we enjoy the work.
- Everything about the answer was positive and upbeat. The candidate talked about solving challenges, rather than dealing with problems.
- The focus was on being part of a successful team, and how the candidate's contributions help teams do well.

Answer framework

Be honest and enthusiastic.

For this question, you want to be honest about the things that you enjoy doing. This is a chance to convince the interviewer that you are a "natural" for the job, or for them to realize that you really won't enjoy doing the job.

Keep it in context.

Make sure to frame these activities so that they align with the job description. Always try to connect your answers back to the role.

Tips

- Use words that convey positive emotions to describe yourself.
- Focus as much on team relationships as your own personal attributes, since a Project Manager can only be successful if the team is successful.
- Be authentic. When you talk about the things that you enjoy, your body language should naturally convey your enthusiasm.

Q10- Tell me about the best project you have ever worked on.

Interviewers want you to open up and tell stories so that they can get to know you. This question gives you a chance to tell a success story that will give the interviewer insights into your experience. It will also give them clues about the things that give you a sense of accomplishment.

Candidate answer and feedback
By Project Manager Professional

Last year, I was on a project team to move our headquarters into a new building. That project basically affected everyone in the company. There were so many things to think about — from the logistics of moving desks and chairs, to reconfiguring the information technology and getting all of the computers and phones online.

Our team got to interact with lots of different people in the company, and with a lot of our vendors and contractors. I learned so much during that project, and really gained a lot of respect for the expertise and insights that all of those people contributed to creating and executing our plan.

It was particularly interesting to see how important communication was in the whole process. There were times when people would miss an email, and it would create a lot of confusion and frustration. So, we all realized that it was really important to focus on keeping the group updated.

There were also a bunch of last minute issues that we had to deal with during the move, like finding some furniture that had been mislabeled. But when it was all done, and we had the grand opening for the new office, it was so rewarding to see how we accomplished a huge, complicated goal by working together. And the folks on the team really became friends during the process.

Why this answer worked well:

- The candidate used a story that was easy to relate to and visualize.
- The answer emphasized the importance of communication, collaboration, and learning from colleagues.
- The candidate showed maturity in dealing with surprises and miscommunications, while maintaining healthy personal relationships.

Answer framework

Choose an example of success

You want to show enthusiasm for working on successful projects.
It's great if you have worked on a project in a company that you
can use as an example. But if you're in school or a recent graduate,
you can use an example from school, volunteering, or even your
family.

Focus on your role

No matter what project you choose to use as your example,
emphasize the key elements of project management as you tell the
story. For example, who were the stakeholders, how did you
develop the plan, how did you maintain communications during
the project, and what did you learn from the experience?

Share what was most gratifying

Emphasize the aspects of the project that made it a great
experience for you. For example, many project managers enjoy the
satisfaction of working with teams to set and accomplish big goals.

Tips

- Build rapport with your interviewer by telling a story that
  you're genuinely excited about that will trigger positive
  emotions and body language.
- Help the interviewer relate to your experience.
- Highlight aspects that might be similar to the job for which
  you are interviewing.
- Don't dwell on jargon or details about the project that will
  be meaningless or irrelevant for the person listening to your
  answer.

Q11- What project management methods are you familiar with?

Interviewers want to know how you manage projects, and how easy it will be for you to work with their teams. Technology companies tend to use Agile project management. Engineering and construction companies usually use a Waterfall approach. Knowing about the company and the industry can help you tailor the answer to this question.

Candidate answer and feedback
By Project Manager Professional

Most of the projects that I have worked on have been software projects where we used Agile and released new software versions every week or two using sprints.

I have also worked on Waterfall projects. I'm trained as a Lean 6 Sigma Blackbelt, so I'm familiar with the DMAIC and DMEDI approaches, and many quality improvement tools.

I have also participated in Gemba Walks and Kaizen events where I worked with a team to identify and implement process improvements. I have also read about the PRINCE2 method, but have not used it in any of the projects that I've worked on.

Why this answer worked well:

- The answer showed that the candidate has an in-depth experience with the Waterfall approach, and a solid working knowledge of other methodologies.
- The answer included keywords that demonstrated familiarity with technical jargon.
- The candidate showed a personal interest and initiative to learn more about project management techniques.

Answer framework

Focus on breadth and depth

There are several different approaches to project management, some of which are more popular in different industries, or for different types of projects. Ideally, it would be good to be familiar with all of them.

Connect your methods to the role

Do your research to find out which methods are being used in the company that you're interviewing with, and which methods they want to use in the future. Some of the most common project management methods are Waterfall, Agile, 6 Sigma, Lean, and PRINCE2.

Tips

- If you know which techniques are important to the interviewer and the role you're applying, make sure you cover those.
- Tailor your response to your audience. It's fine to demonstrate your technical knowledge by including specific industry terms for the appropriate interviewers. Just don't overdo it.

Q12- Imagine that you need to clarify the roles and responsibilities of the team members on a project you're managing. What tools could help you do this?

An interviewer wants to see whether you know how and when to use common project management tools. This question goes beyond describing a tool, and asks for you to analyze a common situation and apply the right tools to help you resolve it.

Candidate answer and feedback
By Project Manager Professional

One of the easiest ways to clarify roles and responsibilities for any project team is to create a RACI Matrix.

The RACI Matrix would help me understand which team members are responsible or accountable for a task, or whether they need to be consulted or informed. This helps to streamline the work, avoid confusion, and ensure that communication is focused for maximum productivity.

This would also help me understand who I need to talk with for status updates, as well as where I would go when issues arise.

Finally, this would help each of my team members feel confident in their understanding of their roles and responsibilities so the project can ultimately be successful.

Why this answer worked well:

- The candidate shared the tool that experienced Project Managers most often use to address the challenge of clarifying roles and responsibilities.
- The candidate went beyond answering the question, and showed an understanding of how the RACI matrix is built.
- The answer was framed in terms of the benefits to the team.

Answer framework

Acknowledge the importance of having responsibilities clearly defined

Share that you understand that clarifying roles and responsibilities is a common challenge in projects. This is an opportunity to demonstrate your skill in evaluating what each team member needs to do in order for the project to be successful.

Use the RACI Matrix

Detail your knowledge of this popular project management tool and how it helps teams. A RACI matrix helps define projects roles and responsibilities through the following components:

Responsible: the team member who does the work.

Accountable: the team member who delegates work and reviews the final outcome.

Consulted: team members who add expertise to strengthen the project.

Informed: team members who are kept in the loop at a high level throughout the project.

Tips

- Be prepared for questions about specific project management tools.
- Share your understanding of how these tools work, how to build them, and why they are useful.

Q13- Imagine that I am your supervisor, and I'm putting you in charge of launching a new project. The project lends itself to a traditional waterfall approach. What should you do next?

The interviewer wants to see if you know where to start when managing a project. This is a great opportunity for you to describe how you would apply your knowledge and experience to take on a new project, and set it up for success.

Candidate answer and feedback
By Project Manager Professional

First, I'm going to ask you a few questions and create a project charter so that we clearly understand your goals for the project, and why you think Waterfall is the best method.

Based on the charter, I'll start reaching out to the people who will be involved in the project so that we can define requirements and create a plan. Once the project kicks off, I'll make sure that we're tracking everyone's tasks and their status.

We'll create a scorecard that's updated every week, showing the work that was completed and any issues that have come up. And, we'll make sure that everyone knows what they need to work on next, and when it needs to be completed.

I'll also make sure that we have a communication plan, a scope change approval process, and a plan in place to capture our lessons learned.

Why this answer worked well:

- The candidate demonstrated an understanding of the considerations when starting a project, including goals and stakeholders.
- The candidate explained that their approach would keep the sponsor informed and involved.

- The answer showed that the candidate can build healthy relationships, and get the project done.

Answer framework

Think like a supervisor

Try to put yourself in the role of the supervisor, and imagine the perfect employee. You'd want someone who has the know-how and independence to catch the ball and run with it, keep you in the loop, and warn you about problems before they become serious.

Answer with confidence

Show the interviewer that you know how to get the right people involved, ask the right questions, create a plan, and deal with issues that come up along the way.

Tips

- Remember that the interviewer is looking for your technical knowledge, as well as your professional maturity, business acumen, and emotional intelligence.
- Share your ability to use influence and authority to engage project stakeholders.
- Focus on your organizational and communication skills.

Q14- What experience do you have in our industry?

Having industry-specific experience can help you understand important things like technical jargon, business structures, and regulatory requirements. Interviewers want to know whether you have this kind of knowledge already, because it can help you be more effective.

Candidate answer and feedback
By Project Manager Professional

I've been using your company's products for years and am a big fan of the brand.

I also spent time working for one of your suppliers, so I understand the focus that your company has on quality and reliability. When I was in school, we spent a lot of time learning about the challenges facing this industry because of new technologies and changing consumer expectations.

I also understand the company's complex supply chain, with customers and suppliers spread all over the world. So, I'm sure that there's a lot more to learn.

That said, I'm confident in my basic understanding of major trends, and how you're actively responding to maintain your competitive advantage.

Why this answer worked well:

- The candidate shared their relevant knowledge and an interest in learning.
- The answer included a combination of practical experience and academic learning.
- The candidate highlighted the importance of where the company is positioned within its industry.

Answer framework

Think broadly about experience

If you have worked in a similar company before, then detail that work history. Keep in mind, being a customer or a supplier to the industry could be relevant experience.

Highlight parallels and education

If you don't have prior experience in the industry, then you can try to draw connections to other experiences. Also, you can compensate for formal work experience by showing that you have studied the industry, either in school or on your own.

Tips

- The more you know about the industry, the easier it is to talk candidly with the interviewer about their business
- Depending on the role for which you are interviewing, industry knowledge could be a "nice-to-have" or an "essential requirement".
- Prepare for your interview by reading articles in relevant publications to get a sense for the industry dynamics, jargon, and current issues. Publicly traded companies publish shareholder reports that can be very informative.

Q15- Tell me about a time you worked on a project in our industry.

This is a way for the interviewer to get insights about your experience working in their industry. This can be especially important for roles where an understanding of technology platforms, industry standards, or government regulations are necessary.

Candidate answer and feedback
By Project Manager Professional

Last year, I was hired as a project coordinator for a commercial construction company across town. As the prime contractor, we had to coordinate the schedules for our subcontractors, clients, labor unions, and government inspectors.

There were several situations that arose over the course of the project that required us to to adjust our plans. For example, we encountered weather issues and material shortages. In these situations, it was really important to figure out who would be affected, so that we could work together to come up with a solution.

One of the biggest lessons that I learned from that experience is the importance of getting accurate information quickly, and then sharing it with the people who need to know to keep things progressing in the right direction.

Why this answer worked well:

- This answer showed that the candidate understands who the stakeholders are for projects in this industry, and how important it is to work effectively with all of them.
- The candidate demonstrated an understanding of the risks that projects in this industry often face, as well as their approach to dealing with them when they occur.
- The answer provided hooks for the interviewer to go deeper with follow-up questions, creating the opportunity to turn the

interview into more of a friendly conversation. For example, the interviewer might follow up by asking, "Was your project affected by that big tornado last summer?"

Answer framework

Show that you've done your homework

Your goal with this question is to show that you are knowledgeable about the industry in which this company sits. Of course, this question will be a lot easier if you have previous experience working in the same industry.

Draw parallels and highlight experience

Even if you don't have experience in the industry, you can show that you understand how the industry works, and why your education and experience would be a good fit.

Tips

- Use this question as an opportunity to share your knowledge of their business, and the dynamics of their industry.
- Prepare by reading trade journals from the industry, and make note of the themes, trends, and key terms.
- Drop a little industry jargon to look like a pro. Just be sure that you really understand what you are saying.

Made in United States
Troutdale, OR
04/30/2024

19553520R00024